MIRACLES

Ronald Knox

1927

CATHOLIC TRUTH SOCIETY

PUBLISHERS TO THE HOLY SEE

Ronald Knox (1888-1957) was a Catholic priest,
translator of the Bible, and renowned spiritual writer.

CTS ONEFIFTIES

First published 1927.

Published by The Incorporated Catholic Truth Society,

40-46 Harleyford Road, London SE11 5AY

www.ctsbooks.org

ISBN 978 1 78469 532 3

Miracles are a message addressed from God to man… they have all one primary purpose, and that is to be an evidence of his Almighty Power.

MIRACLES

Ronald Knox

I.—THE POSSIBILITY OF MIRACLES

There is a significant story to be found in one
of the less familiar by-ways of Old Testament
history. When Israel had been oppressed for seven
years under the tyrannous yoke of the Midianites,
God would raise up a deliverer for His people;
and His choice fell upon Gedeon, a hero of little
estimation, till then, in the world's eyes; "Behold,"
he says, "my family is the meanest in Manasses,
and I am the least in my father's house." Humility,
rather than want of faith, made Gedeon ask for a
sign, a miraculous sign, that this strange vocation
was really meant for him. And Almighty God saw
fit to indulge his request. Gedeon laid a fleece of
wool on the ground, and left it there all night. The
first night the fleece alone was wet with dew, when
all the ground was dry; the next night, the fleece
alone was dry, and there was dew on all the ground.
An unfamiliar incident, and one which would

hardly be remembered by ordinary Christian folk but for the providential accident that it serves us for a type of our Blessed Lady's Child-bearing; she, like Gedeon's fleece, was the one spot in our benighted and parched world where the dew of Divine Grace could find a lodgement, when in the fulness of time we were set free from the tyranny of our sins.

I say, a significant story, because it seems to me that it throws into relief a very important consideration which we are apt to overlook when we discuss the subject of miracles. What consideration? Why, this—that those special exercises of Divine power which we call miracles are not in themselves greater, are not in themselves more sensational, are not in themselves more deserving of our gratitude than His ordinary operations in nature. It was a wonderful sight, doubtless, when after a sleepless night spent between hope and self-distrust, Gedeon went out at dawn to find the fleece wringing wet, glistening like silver in the grey light of morning. And yet, when he went out the next day, was there not a still more wonderful vision awaiting him? A whole world silvered with dew, diamonds shining from every blade of grass and every fallen leaf, the very gossamer in the fields a patch-work of filigree? You have seen as much yourself, maybe, on some early summer morning in the country. Oh no, there was nothing wonderful about it, of course; you were quite right; it was just dew… Nothing wonderful, because we're so accustomed to it, because we take it so for granted. When you saw that sight long ago, with the clear eyes of childhood, or with the transfiguring vision of first love, perhaps you caught the marvel of it; and since then, what exactly has happened? Is it that the dew-drenched world is less wonderful? Or that you have lost your faculty of wonder?

It is important to realize that the same power which covered a single fleece with dew one night covered a whole landscape with dew the next night. And which was the marvel? Which shewed the greater exercise of power, which signalized God's bounty in greater profusion? The first night, or the second? Because in the second instance we can account for the phenomenon, whereas in the first instance we cannot account for the phenomenon, we call the first instance a miracle. But if we had not lost the child's faculty of wonder, we should see the same hand at work on the second night as on the first, only with more widespread effect, only with richer largesse. The same hand, the same power, only exercised in a different way. The same power which sent the stars rolling on their courses gives sudden health to some poor cripple at Lourdes, and we say, "Impossible!" The feeding of the Five Thousand, *that* taxes our powers of belief to the utmost. And yet, as St. Augustine pointed out long ago, what is the feeding of the five thousand compared with that patient process by which vast plains of wheat shoot up and bud and mature, under God's hand, to make the slices of bread which you forgot to say grace over yesterday? The same hand, the same power.

A miracle, though it ought to mean any event, natural or super-natural, which claims our wonder, is the term technically applied to a particular class of the wonderful works of God. God ordinarily brings events to pass in the natural world by means of secondary causes. When He suspends for a moment the action of those secondary causes, we call it a miracle. There are those who deny that any event of this kind has ever happened. And their arguments can be conveniently classed under three heads: Can God do miracles? Would God do miracles? And does God do miracles? I am not going to consider at present the question whether, as a matter of fact, miracles have ever happened. I want first to establish two points; that God can do miracles, if He will; and that there are circumstances in which we should expect God to do miracles, if He can.

Can God do miracles? From its very terms, such a question cannot be discussed with those who deny the existence of a deity. But there have been, and are people who are bound to return a negative to that question, because their philosophy has a conception of Almighty God's nature which is altogether different from ours. A century or two ago, it was the Deists who felt bound to deny miracles. To-day, it is the Pantheists who feel bound to deny miracles. Deism was a passing fashion of yesterday, as Pantheism is a passing fashion of to-day. The one is the precise opposite of the other, but what of that? It is the world's way to shift between extremes. The Church looks on with patience; she has seen so many of these changing moods, and she has outlived them all.

The Deists thought of creation as a machine which God had wound up, once for all, and left it to run its course by the inexorable law of its own mechanism. He was, indeed, the First Cause and the Prime Mover, but He did not uphold and govern His creation—he had left it to itself, as a man sets a ball rolling or a top spinning and goes his way. Naturally, such philosophers had to disbelieve in miracle. For a single variation from the unswerving laws by which the natural creation was governed would mean a spoke in the wheel, an interference which must needs set the whole machinery out of gear. The Pantheists of to-day think of Almighty God, rather, as if He were caught up in the wheels of His own machine. He is essential to our existence, says the Pantheist, but then, we in our turn are essential to His. He is to the world what man's soul is to man's body, a spiritual principle which pervades and inspires this mass of material creation. And of course, a God so conceived cannot stand outside His own Creation, cannot exempt Himself, therefore, from its natural laws, which are laws for Him no less than for us; once more, then, miracles must be declared impossible.

We have not time to consider here how grossly inadequate are both those conceptions of God. I will only say of such a God as that, that I would not cross the street to worship him. Those who would shelter themselves under the Christian Name are committed to a very different understanding of the Divine Nature. In the beginning was God; before suns or stars set out upon their course, He existed, eternally independent, eternally Self-sufficing; no room for Pantheism here. And yet, are not two sparrows sold for a farthing? And not one of them shall fall on the ground without your Father—the Deist, no less than the Pantheist, is silenced by the Christian revelation. For us, the Power which made the worlds out of nothing is the Power which still upholds, from day to day, from moment to moment, this vast fabric of Creation; it can experience no effect of which He is not the Cause, it can be stirred by no motion of which He is not the originator. Not one of them shall fall to the ground without your Father—when a sparrow flies against a telegraph wire and falls dead, it is He who supplies the force of its flight, and the resistance with which it meets; His Hand communicates the impact of the shock to the little fluttering heart, and draws the lifeless creature down into the bosom of its parent earth. That is the God we Christians worship.

But, you say, that is nonsense, that is to throw out a silly challenge to the whole world of science. If dew falls on the ground, you say, that is because the moisture with which the air is laden has condensed with the chill of night; that is the cause which produces the effect. The secondary cause, yes; the scientific cause, yes; but none of these secondary causes could operate for a moment without the concurrence of Almighty God. It is the law of gravitation which brings the sparrow to the ground; true enough, yet the law of gravitation itself—what is it but the direct expression of His will? Ordinarily, in all the million details of our daily experience, He works thus, expressing His will through the laws which Science tabulates for us, laws which operate uniformly, no effect without its cause, back to the first amoeba in which life was found, back to the first nebula from which matter took birth—and yet, all the time it is His power, directly exercised, which lends these causes their efficacy. You are puzzled by miracles? I tell you, if you could only recognize the necessity of God's action in the world, the fall of a sparrow to the ground would be ten thousand times more staggering to your poor, finite imagination. It is a thing to make you dream at night, and wake gasping with the wonder of it.

And a miracle—a miracle is a very simple thing by comparison. It happens when, once and again in these long aeons of the world's existence, God expresses His will more directly, by suspending for a moment, at one tiny pin-point of space, the operation of those laws which could have no force and no validity but from Him. Just in the millionth instance God does, without the aid of secondary causes, what He is continually doing by means of secondary causes. Just in the millionth instance He multiplies bread instead of multiplying the wheat. Just in the millionth instance He will have the dew form not everywhere but just *here*. Is that so much of a privilege to claim for the Omnipotent? Is that impossible with God, with such a God?

I may be pardoned for giving a very simple and a very vulgar illustration; I use it reluctantly because I want to bring this point home. There are such people as newspaper proprietors; and some of these proprietors are in the habit of dictating, from day to day, the policy of the papers they own. All the leading articles—we will not speak of the news service—are written by men who are paid to express, in every line they write, the will of a newspaper proprietor. Now, suppose that once in ten years, on some exceptionally important occasion, a newspaper proprietor should write his own leading article. What is he doing? He is doing what he does every day; the only difference is that just this once he is doing directly what he has been doing daily for ten years through the instrumentality of others. That will give some idea of what I mean when I say that the God who operates continually through secondary causes has the right, if He will, to dispense with secondary causes.

But now, granted that God can do miracles, would He do miracles? It has become a fashion, among the more timorous and compromising Protestant theologians of our time, to admit that in the abstract God has the power to do miracles if He would, but to pretend that it is in some way beneath His dignity to do them. The idea of miracles, for their minds, savours too much of a theatrical performance; it suggests, somehow, that the natural Creation with its natural laws is not a perfect one, inasmuch as these natural laws have to be suspended in their operation, from time to time, in face of special emergencies. They do not care to think of the law of gravitation as if it were like some human enactment which on the whole deals out justice, but has occasionally to be mitigated in its operation, where the circumstances are exceptional. Cannot we trust Providence (they say), guiding its own course in accordance with those uniform laws of nature which science discloses to us, to bring out everything for the best, without these violent interruptions, without these sudden reversals of the natural process, which we call miracle?

There is just this much worth in that argument, that it would be, manifestly, derogatory to all our ideas of God's dignity if we supposed that He performed miracles frivolously, capriciously, without sufficient cause. It is only with great misgiving and full consciousness of our limited knowledge that we, His creatures, can presume to guess what God would or would not do. But everything which revelation or natural theology can tell us about the character of God, everything which Science can teach us about the uniformity of Nature, fortifies us in the belief that miracles are a very exceptional feature in God's ordinance of the world, designed to meet exceptional needs. We are not to multiply miracles beyond what is necessary. To take a very simple way of illustrating that, let me suggest that Almighty God would not do a sensible miracle in circumstances where there was nobody there to see or to be conscious of the experience. Miracles are a message from Him addressed to man, they would not occur unless man were present to witness them. I think it is not presuming too much upon our human philosophy to suggest that.

They are a message addressed from God to Man. And, although they may have various secondary purposes—the relief of human pain, the satisfaction of human needs, the vindication of innocence against injustice, and so on—they have all one primary purpose, and that is to be an evidence—if the word had not become vulgarized in our day, I would say an advertisement—of His

Almighty Power. To prove that He does govern the world; to prove that the Catholic Church is His Church, bearing the seal of His commission; to prove that this or that man or woman is a Saint, one of his special friends, and therefore worthy of special honour from the faithful—that is the sort of motive which is a sufficient motive to call this special exercise of His power into play.

But, you say, if miracles are only an evidence of God's power, surely they must be unnecessary? Have we not just agreed that His natural operations are, in themselves, more wonderful even than miracles? Why cannot we be content, then, to learn His Omnipotence from the lightning and from the sunset, from the multitudinous perfections of creation, from the delicate workmanship of leaf and petal, from the patterns which the frost traces on our windows? Having left us such witness of Himself, having set upon our world this seal of creative wisdom, would He do more than that? Would He try to arrest our attention by breaking his own laws, as the more vulgar kind of modern music arrests our attention by working discords into its harmony? Must He sacrifice consistency, to advertise Omnipotence?

The answer to that objection is two-fold. In the first place, God does not do miracles *merely* to display His power, merely to shew that He can do them. He does miracles, because He wants to draw our attention to this or that valuable movement among our fellow-men, to this or that sanctified career. What is more important, than that we should take notice of a Saint? And who is more anxious that we should take no notice of him, than the Saint himself? The very humility of the Saints would defeat God's purpose for them, if He did not take His own steps to shed lustre upon their self-effacing virtues. It is miracle that gives us the assurance: "Behold My servant, whom I have chosen."

And there is this further answer to be made. Doubtless we ought not to need miracles, *but we do*. If Adam had never fallen, perhaps the course of nature would have gone on uninterrupted; sufficient for mankind its daily intimacy with God, its unspoiled admiration of His marvellous works. Nay, even if fallen man had succeeded in maintaining such intimacy, such admiration, perhaps there would have been no need of miracles to catch our wandering attention. But we forget Him so easily, that He has to startle us out of our forgetfulness. So a great artist might trust that the skilfulness of his own painting would be enough warrant of its genuineness; and yet—men are so hesitating, so hard to please! At the last moment he scrawls his PINXIT in the corner. Miracles are God's signature, appended to His masterpiece of creation; not because they ought to be needed, but because they are needed. And if you doubt it, tell me of any religion that has really affected millions of men, really stirred their hearts, that did not claim miracles for its sanction.

Saint John, in the reminiscences which he has left to us of his Master's utterances, has been careful, I think, to preserve for us those which explain why it is perilous for a man to neglect the message of the Gospel. He insists, or rather he reminds us how Our Lord insisted, on the terrible truth that though God became Man in order to save us from our sins, His Coming not only saves; it also condemns. When the claim of Our Lord Jesus Christ becomes clear to a man, it presents him with a formidable alternative. He may accept it, and save his soul. Or he may reject it, and then he is worse off than he would have been if he had never heard the name of Christ. The revelation of Himself which Almighty God gave to the world in the Face of His Incarnate Son is not a thing to be played with. It is a two-edged sword that pierces the hearts of men and divides them into two categories—those who accept and those who reject it.

It follows, surely, from that, that this revelation must be fully accredited, must bear unmistakeable signs of being a direct revelation from God to men. If any room were left for reasonable doubt, then surely He would not be so strict in calling us to account for the hearing we gave it, the welcome we offered to it in our lives. If a Government passes a law which attaches the death penalty to some particular form of wrong-doing, it will be careful above all things that the promulgation of this law is attended with every possible circumstance of solemnity. It must be published in official form, in official language, the seal of the Sovereign himself must be attached to it for all to see. Otherwise, men might excuse themselves for disobeying the law on the ground that they doubted whether the proclamation was genuine or a forgery. So, when God gave us His revelation, with all the terrible responsibility it involved for human souls, He would not leave its genuineness in doubt. He put his seal upon it, and that seal was miracle. If I had not done among them the works that no other man hath done, they would not have sin; but now, now that they have seen My miracles and nevertheless rejected Me, they have both seen and hated both Me and My Father.

So Our Lord said of His contemporaries. And now, what of us, to whom the story of those mighty works comes down as a memory from the distant past, a faint echo in history? There is one very stupid thing which is constantly said on this subject, which we had better examine at once.

You will hear people say, "We, in our day, believe the Gospel in spite of the miracles it records, not because of them. To us, miracles make it harder, not easier, to accept the Christian faith." Now, if you examine that statement for a moment, you will see that it rests on a very silly confusion. In order to believe the Gospel, you must do two things. You must first of all convince yourself that the narrative which the Evangelists have left us is true; and then you must decide whether the Church is right in inferring, from the narrative, that the Hero of the story was Incarnate God. Now, it's quite true to say that the miracles which are recorded in the Gospel don't make it easier for us to believe *in the truth of the narrative.* But then, who ever thought they would? Who ever, in his wildest dreams, imagined that a document was MORE likely to be historically accurate because it represented its Hero as walking on the water, instead of walking on the land? The suggestion is ridiculous. No, the value of miracle comes in when we reach the second process, the process of proving that the Church is right in representing the Hero of the Gospels as Incarnate God. Now, is anybody going to be such a fool as to tell us that miracles make it harder for us, instead of easier for us, to believe that? Is anybody going to say: "What! Did Christ walk on the water? Then of course He can't have been God! Did Christ rise from the dead? Then of course He can't have been God?" Obviously, if the Gospels give us satisfactory evidence that our Lord walked on the water and rose from the dead, then that is the best possible proof that the claim He made was true.

I will go further, and say it is the only *adequate* proof that His claim was true. I will not speak dogmatically here; I will simply record my own religious state of mind. I will simply say that if it were not for the miracles which the Gospel records (including among those the fulfilment of Old Testament prophecies) I would not, personally, be a Christian. I should think it a treachery to my reason to accept the divine claim of an unmiraculous Christ. I know that there are people who will tell you that even if Our Lord had done no miracles on earth they would have accepted, and would have felt bound to accept, His assertion of His own Deity. For myself, I could not accept it, and should think the worse of others if they did.

But, you say, was it not enough for Our Lord's contemporaries to see His face enlightened by a charity not of this world, to hear His gracious speech, to watch His unfailing meekness and patience, His sympathy with the poor and the outcast? With such evidence before their eyes, was it not their duty to hail Him as a God? Theirs perhaps; but mine? No artist has put on record for me, even if I could trust the skill of artists, that heavenly beauty of which you speak; the accents of that gracious speech had faded from the world before my living memory; the record of His actions which is left to us is very far from complete, and, at this distance of years, it is not different in kind from other records of sanctity, the record of St. Francis, the record of St. Philip Neri. It is a biography to which even the most cynical of readers is bound to pay homage, as the story of an amazing human career; but do we dare to say that the Hero of it is self-evidently God?

But at least (you insist) if that living revelation of a human Character which was enough for His contemporaries is not enough for you, sundered from it as you are by the centuries and by the changing fashions of human thought, have not His own words been put on record for you; and do not *they* attest His Divinity? "Never man spoke like this man" that was the verdict of His audience, and has not the written word power to move our hearts as well? Once more I say, they are words whose spiritual beauty even scoffers have recognized, even His enemies have been unable to traduce. But is there anything He said which a merely human Teacher *could not* have said? And, even if you tell me that the words themselves bear the hallmark of a Divine origin, is it not perfectly possible that God may have chosen a merely human Prophet for His mouthpiece? That He who spoke through Moses spoke through Jesus Christ? What evidence, then, that this unique Spokesman of Almighty God was himself Divine?

But stay—there is a point we have overlooked. This unique historical Figure, Jesus of Nazareth, whose Life was so transparently holy, whose reported utterances are such a store-house of heavenly wisdom, did CLAIM to be God. We cannot think of such a Prophet as a conscious impostor; to write Him down a madman, the victim of a hallucination, would be false to the whole picture which our records give of Him: you cannot associate delusions or hysteria with such a Personality as this! Why then, if He said He was God, He must have been God; there is no other way to it…I know; that argument is frequently used. God forgive me if I am putting difficulties in anybody's way, but it seems to me that it carries weight as an indication, yet stops short of proof. And we demand, remember, nothing less than proof; He Himself, this Hero of the Gospels, puts forth an absolute claim; to refuse it is not merely to miss a spiritual opportunity, but to involve yourself in a condemnation; He claims, then, to have proved His case. And the notion that unique spiritual gifts are compatible with delusions, and even with hysteria, may be a very improbable, but it is not a strictly impossible notion. The whole history of religious enthusiasm bears witness that the highest sanctity often runs on the very border-lines of sanity. To write down Jesus of Nazareth as a deluded fanatic is bad history, I grant you. But if you cut the miraculous out of the story, it is not impossible history.

How, then, was God to reveal himself? What further seal could He set upon the earthly Mission of his Only-begotten Son? There was nothing that He could do, except to usher in His coming by catastrophies of nature; that is, by miracle. And there are two more points in this connexion which are not remembered as carefully as they deserve to be.

In the first place, Our Lord did not come to earth unexpected and unannounced; He made no sudden intrusion into our world. He came to people who had been taught to expect His coming; their prophets, long ago, had looked forward to a Deliverer who should save His people from their sins. When He came, the eyes of the blind were to be opened, the ears of the deaf were to be unstopped; the lame man should leap as an hart, and the tongue of the dumb should sing. That means that the Messiah who was expected was a Messiah who should come with miracle. And that was the popular expectation of Our Lord's own day. "When the Christ comes," they said, "will He do more miracles than these?" The Jews were expecting, and expecting with justice, a miraculous Messiah. Did Christ come to them without miracle, and condemn them for rejecting Him?

Another point. Our Lord Himself claimed to do miracles, and pointed to His miracles as the evidence of His Divinity. "If I had not done among them the works that no other man hath done, they would not have sin." "Or else believe me for the very works' sake." And, in answer to John's question whether He were the Messiah, "Go and tell John what you see and hear; the blind see, the lame walk, the lepers are cleansed, the deaf hear." And to the Pharisees "If I by the finger of God cast out devils, then doubtless the kingdom of God is come among you." And above all, He pointed forward to the crowning miracle of His Resurrection. Deliberately He flung out a challenge to His critics; let them kill Him, and

He would prove them in the wrong by triumphing over death. "Destroy this temple, and in three days I will raise it up." "No sign shall be given to this generation but the sign of Jonas the prophet. For as Jonas was three days and three nights in the whale's belly, so shall the Son of Man be in the heart of the earth three days and three nights." And repeatedly, when He foretold His Passion to His disciples, He foretold that on the third day He would rise again. He issued a challenge; and if He never fulfilled the terms of that challenge, if it was only some pale Ghost that left the Tomb on Easter morning, can He blame us, can He condemn us, if we fail to believe?

I say, then, that if ever there was an occasion when it was antecedently probable that God would signalize His Almighty power by miracle, it was here. A revelation came from Him which claimed to be an unmistakable revelation; and it could not be unmistakable, unless it were accompanied by miracle. He had foretold it through His prophets, and had foretold that it would be accompanied by miracle. Finally, He who came to make that revelation pointed to His miraculous powers as evidence of His Divinity. And now, what are the historical facts?

We have four records of the Incarnate Life in question. Everybody admits that they were all in circulation a hundred years or so after the events they record; that two of them at least were in circulation forty years after the events they record. Three of them at least were written by simple men who set out merely to report the facts which they had witnessed with their own eyes or heard from eyewitnesses; had no theological thesis to defend, no theories to maintain. There is no conceivable reason why those records should not be accepted as unreservedly as, let us say, Caesar's commentaries. No reason whatever, except one. They report miracles.

They tell us, that the Hero of their story was not born according to the wont of man; He was conceived in the Womb of a pure Virgin. As He went about the earth, He was not content to cure sicknesses by a power that could be mistaken for faith-healing; He walked upon the water, He multiplied five loaves to feed five thousand, He changed water into wine. Murdered by His enemies, He rose from the dead the third day, and the very Tomb in which His Body had been laid was found, the third day, a cenotaph. That is the story which these records tell, in the same calm, dispassionate accents in which Caesar chronicles his military operations.

Where they report miracles, in so far as they report miracles, these records are discredited by the critics of to-day—why? BECAUSE they report miracles. Was there ever such madman's logic? We prove to them that Almighty God can do miracles. We prove to them that He is likely to do miracles, given sufficient cause. We prove to them that the revelation of Himself which He made to the world not merely gave sufficient cause for miracles, but demanded miracles if it was to be a revelation at all. And then we say, Here are the miracles; here is the record of them. And they say, Oh, but we can't accept that record. Indeed, we say, and why not? Why not? (they answer) Oh, because it reports miracles.

Of course, if you found a chapter in Caesar's commentaries which purported to describe how Caesar fed the Tenth Legion with five loaves and two fishes, you would do right to suspect that that chapter was spurious. Not because miracles are impossible, but because in such a case the conditions are absent which make miracles probable. Caesar made no claim to supernatural powers, needed no argument, save the sword, to support his authority. But the Gospels deal with a situation in which miracles are not only natural; they are necessary. Our Lord was not claiming that He was merely a prophet, was not claiming that He was merely a man entrusted with a divine mission. He was claiming that He had been personally present when the foundations of the earth were laid, when the morning stars sang their praises together, and all the sons of God made a joyful melody. He was claiming that He had existed from all eternity, the Co-equal Word of the Omnipotent Father. Was He to prove this by earnest moral exhortations, by devoted missionary zeal, by patient endurance of indignities? Put Raphael down at a street-corner as a pavement-artist, what proof can he give of his identity but to paint like Raphael? Bring God down to earth, what proof can He give of His Godhead but to command the elements like God?

Don't mistake me; I don't mean to deny, or to underestimate, the moral witness of Our Lord's life, His kindness, His gentleness, His patience, His indignation against human wrongs. Without that moral witness, a string of reported miracles would not have sufficed to convince us that here indeed was God come down to earth. But that moral witness, by itself, though it may be a sufficient basis for the namby-pamby theologies of to-day, would not be an adequate proof of Godhead if it were not combined with the witness of Our Lord's miracles. In Power *and* in Goodness God is made known to us by His creation; and when He came to make Himself known to us afresh by His Incarnation the same twofold seal was required. Man was to recognize, beyond all possibility of excuse, that the two revelations shewed the master-stroke of the same Artist's hand. To know and to reject Jesus Christ was to have seen and to have hated both Him and His Heavenly Father.

III.—MIRACLE IN THE HISTORY
OF THE CHURCH

In the Old Testament passage to which I have already referred, Gedeon is represented as asking, "Where are God's miracles, of which our fathers have told us? But now the Lord hath forsaken us." It seemed to him, as he looked round him at the miserable servitude of his fellow-countrymen, that somehow Almighty God either could not or would not stretch out His hand to send miraculous deliverance to His people, as He had stretched forth His hand long ago, when Moses brought them out of Egypt. It was a doubt that presented itself constantly to the Jewish people, and you will find a similar doubt in the Christian Church at almost every stage of her history. Pious people will say nowadays, "How I wish I had lived in the Middle Ages, when miracles were constantly happening! One knows they happen nowadays, but they are so rare!" Well, if you will read the Dialogues of St. Gregory, written just about six hundred years after Our Lord's birth, just at the time when England was being converted to the Christian faith, you will find that the monk Peter raises exactly the same difficulty. Why are we so apt to make that complaint? Partly, I think, because it is our constant habit to think others better off than ourselves. Partly because Divine Providence works miracles where it will and when it will, not according to our preconceived notions of what is fitting or probable.

But always—remember this—always the Catholic Church has believed in miracles, not as something that used to happen a long time ago in Palestine, but as something that may happen anywhere, any day, given the proper conditions. And if you are arguing with some High Church objector about Continuity, and want to make him see that the Church of England after the Reformation was not the same thing as the Church of England before the Reformation, here is a good rough test. The reformed Church of England lost at once, and lost for several centuries, and has, for the most part, never recovered the Catholic instinct about miracles. The old-fashioned Anglicans used to believe in miracles happening up to 60 A.D.; they had to, because it was in the Bible. But any miracle reported since that date they put down at once as a monkish fable. They did not accept miracles, did not expect miracles, did not want miracles. They had lost, you see, that instinct which we Catholics have that we are the spoilt children of Almighty

God—that we never know when we may not have a surprise present in store for us.

And so they took to insisting on that rather clumsy distinction between Bible miracles and ecclesiastical miracles. There is, of course, a distinction between the two; we are bound to believe in the Bible miracles, because they are in the Bible; we are not bound as Catholics to believe in this or that miracle of later times. We're bound to believe that St. Peter the Apostle walked on the water, because the Gospel tells us that he did. We are not *bound* to believe that St. Peter of Alcantara walked across a river dry-shod, although that story is told of him. But in this discussion I have taken the liberty of dividing my subject not into Bible miracles and ecclesiastical miracles, but into Gospel miracles and ecclesiastical miracles. We have considered the miracles which Our Lord did Himself, during His lifetime. We have to consider now the miracles which He has done and still does through the agency of His Saints, now that His feet tread no longer the ways of our earth. Unless from a mere prejudice not founded on reason you deny all possibility of miracle, the Gospel miracles need no justification. Obviously, if there was ever a moment at which miracles were likely to occur, it was when the Incarnate Son of God came into the world. How else could Almighty God have set His seal on His own revelation, marked it out unmistakably from every other human event, except by wonders and by signs? But there was no reason in the nature of the case why these manifestations should have gone on after Our Lord's Ascension into heaven. We might have expected, even, that since this revelation was unique and final, so the manifestation of divine power which accompanied it would have been unique and final—no more walking on the water, no more rising from the dead. But as a matter of fact, if you turn to the Acts of the Apostles, you find yourself confronted with miracle. If you turn to St. Paul's epistles, you find him justifying his own apostolic position by appealing to miracle. And wherever you turn in reading the lives of the Saints, from John the Evangelist in the first century to John Vianney in the nineteenth, you will spoil the whole lesson of them and lose the whole flavour of them if you try to leave out of sight this miraculous element in the story.

Our Lord foretold it Himself, just before His Ascension. These signs shall follow them that believe; In My name they shall cast out devils; they shall speak with new tongues, they shall take up serpents, and if they drink any deadly thing, it shall not hurt them. They shall lay their hands on the sick, and they shall recover. Really, the pious Christian who reads those words might more reasonably wonder why there are so few miracles than why there are any miracles at all. We might wonder why every Ordination is not accompanied by the visible fiery tongues of Pentecost, why every beggar at every church door is not healed of his infirmities like the lame man at the Beautiful Gate. But we find, as a matter of history and as a matter of common experience, that these signs are only vouchsafed by Almighty God at distant and irregular intervals, for the most part in connexion with the lives and deaths of men and women of recognizable holiness. We take the facts as we find them; we admit that miracles are not common. We admit that stories of miracles have to be accepted with reserve, and the evidence for them carefully weighed. But we do not admit that miracles never happen. We refuse to admit that, because it happens to be clean contrary to the evidence.

Of course, admirers of the Reformation will give you a very different account of the matter. They will tell you that the medieval mind was child-like, unscientific, and fond of fairy-tales; when the human race came to its maturity in the sixteenth century, the fairy-tales were put away. We of the modern world can only look back upon those fables with the affected interest which grown-up people take in a doll's house. For us, science has made it impossible to believe in miracles. We do not blame the medieval mind; but we cannot share, any longer, that unquestioning faith with which our ancestors used to accept stories of the supernatural. Science, they say, half-regretfully, has made that impossible.

To talk like that is to talk arrant nonsense. It is to talk as if the medieval world was not surprised by miracles—but it *was*; that is why it called them miracles. True, our ancestors thought the sun went round the earth, whereas we know that the earth goes round the sun. But they believed that the sun ALWAYS went round the earth, every day, regularly, like clockwork; always the same way, from East to West. If the sun had risen in the West one morning, Dante or St. Francis would have been just as much surprised as you or I would be. You see, they believed just as we do in the uniformity of nature. They believed that in the ordinary course of things every effect has a cause, and every cause is bound to produce its effect unless some hindrance from outside interferes with it. Every effect produced by a cause, back to the remote origins of this material universe,—that was their belief, as it is ours.

And if it had not been, they could not have believed in miracle. All this talk of an opposition between science and miracle is the merest hypocrisy. The fact is that you cannot believe in a miracle unless you believe in science. Supposing you saw a man suddenly lifted up two feet in the air. When you had satisfied yourself that it was not done by wires or mirrors, what verdict would you pass on the performance? Only two verdicts are possible. One is to say, "Why, this must be a miracle! That man is a solid body, and like all solid bodies he is attracted towards the earth's centre. No natural obstacle is counteracting the law of attraction; no scientific explanation is possible; it must, therefore, be a miracle." That is one possible attitude; and the other possible attitude is this, to say "There! I knew it! These scientists do not know their job! Here have they been telling me for years that a solid body is attracted towards the centre of the earth, by a fixed law of nature; and now I can see for myself that it is not true. A solid body is just as likely to rise in the air as not. Henceforth, no science for me; I will not believe in a word the fellows say." Which of those two attitudes is the more respectful towards science? The attitude which can witness a miracle, and still preserve its faith in Sir Isaac Newton? Or the attitude which calls Sir Isaac Newton a liar because once, in exceptional circumstances, his principle, valid in itself, has been superseded by a higher principle?

The exception proves the rule. To recognize that the exception IS an exception proclaims your confidence in the rule. If I say, "What a monstrous thing that Judge Jeffreys should have passed such iniquitous sentences!" am I casting aspersions on the administration of British Law? On the contrary, I am paying a great compliment to the administration of British law, by exclaiming at the injustice of Jeffreys as something monstrous, something exceptional. And in the same way, if I say, "What an extraordinary thing that this man, who has been given up by all the doctors, should be cured at Lourdes!" I am not casting aspersions on the medical faculty. On the contrary, I am paying a compliment to the medical faculty by proclaiming that a cure which took place in defiance of their best diagnosis must obviously be a miraculous cure. Mr. Bernard Shaw is one of the few Agnostics who have a consistent attitude about miracle. He does not believe in miracles, but then he does not believe in Science either. It does not impress him if a man who is despaired of by the doctors recovers at Lourdes, because it is a fixed article of his creed that doctors do not know their job. You cannot acclaim a miraculous cure without believing in the principles of medicine. You cannot cry out in astonishment at a miracle of levitation unless you believe in the law of gravitation.

In fact, what makes it difficult for us to believe in miracles is not human science; it is human nescience. A man is cured at Lourdes who for years has been, to all appearances, a paralytic. It is an answer to prayer. If the paralysis was real, genuine, organic, then the cure was a miracle. If the man was in fact a hysterical patient, if, all the time, it was no organic disturbance, but some obstinate nervous obsession that kept him chained to his bed until the shock of that vast assembly in the great Square drove him to his feet, then it was not a miracle, it was only a special Providence. And we cannot tell which—why? Because the doctors cannot tell us whether the man was, in the first instance, a hysterical patient or no. It is not Our Lady who is at fault, it is the doctors. Their tests are not accurate enough to be able to tell us whether Almighty God, in this particular act of healing, has used natural causes or supernatural causes. It is not human science, it is scientific ignorance, which has created the difficulty.

We do not resent scientific investigation into our stories of miracle; rather, we welcome it. We do not say that in a given case miracle is theologically certain; we only say that it is, so far, the best account we can give of the facts. We differ from our critics only in this, that we say, "It may be a miracle, or it may not," whereas they say, "Whatever it is, it certainly is not a miracle." Which side approaches the subject with an open mind, and in a spirit of enquiry? Which side approaches the subject encumbered with the burden of dogmatic prepossessions? Which side faces the facts?

It is possible that people who dislike the supernatural actually cannot see evidence for it when it is there? That, at least, seems to be the only explanation of a statement; like the statement attributed to Matthew Arnold: "The worst of miracles is that they don't happen." *But they do.* Search heaven and earth if you will for natural explanations of the fact; but don't sit still in your arm-chair and deny the fact; if you do that, you are a case for the alienist. The attitude of these people towards miracle is like the farmer who was taken to the Zoo and said, when they shewed him the giraffe, "There's no such animal." Equally dogmatic, equally unreasoning, is the bigotry of the man who tells you that miracles do not happen, without having once in his life taken the trouble to find out whether they happen or not.

We still measure electricity by volts and amps; Volta and Ampère were convinced Catholics. Mendel, the pioneer of all the study of heredity, was a monk. Pasteur died clasping the Crucifix. With such children as these we Catholics share our nursery and our fairy-stories.

IV.—"MIRACLES" OUTSIDE THE CHURCH

Let us imagine ourselves, for a moment, privileged to witness the greatest of Our Lord's temptations, when the Devil took Him up to the temple roof.

What a spectacle the streets of Jerusalem present, as they are watched from that pinnacle of the temple—watched, alternately, by the leer of Satanic malice, and by the indulgent regard of all-embracing Love! Men swarming everywhere, buying and selling, haggling, gesticulating, begging, praying, cursing, what a panorama! And these pitiful creatures we are watching, dwarfed like ants by the perspective, are God's chosen people, singled out from among all the nations of the earth. These are the men who have been found worthy to receive the Divine Oracles, to see the Son of God Himself walking in their streets. The holy City—I think this is the only occasion on which Jerusalem is so called in the New Testament. The holy City, and these are its holy inhabitants! And then the temptation comes. Can nothing be done to awaken those souls, so bent on worldly aims, to eternal issues? Can nothing turn those earth-bound eyes heavenwards, startle and dazzle those dull hearts into faith? You could do it surely, You, the Son of God, strong in the power of that forty days' fast which lies behind You; You in whom the spirit has already triumphed over the body! Suppose You were to take one step forward, a single step would do it, and let Yourself fall? There would be a startled cry from beneath, hands would point, and eyes would look heavenwards. And then—a miracle! Of course there would be a miracle; You are the Son of God: would He allow His own Son to be dashed in pieces by a fall? Those crowds would then recognize You for what You are, a Messenger from heaven. Try it, why not? Can it be that You doubt God's Providence? That You imagine He could fail You?

Don't misunderstand our Lord's answer. "Thou shalt not tempt the Lord thy God"—that does not mean "Thou, Satan, shalt not tempt Me, Jesus, thy God." It means "I, Jesus of Nazareth, must not tempt, must not make trial of, the Lord My God." Tempting Providence, that is what the text forbids; thrusting yourself into a position of danger and then defying Providence to neglect you, demanding, and depending upon, a miracle. This challenge, which here comes to Our Lord from the Prince of Evil himself, came to Him later from His human enemies, when they tempted Him, demanding of Him a sign from heaven. They wanted Him, as Satan wanted Him, to do miracles to order. They offered Him the grudging tribute of their belief on condition that He should shew them a portent; He refused. Once again, when He was led away from Pilate to Herod in the hour of His Passion, He could have saved Himself if He would have gratified Herod's curiosity by performing a miracle; once more He refused. Incarnate God will shew His power where He wills and as He wills, not to meet our incredulous challenge, not in answer to our want of faith.

What Our Lord did, He did for our instruction. And you will find a mirror of His instruction in the Catholic attitude about miracle. The Catholic Church believes in miracle, hopes for miracle, encourages her children to pray, if they will, for miracle. But you must not, she says, demand miracle. You must not tempt God, try to force His hand, throw yourself into danger and challenge Him, for His own honour, to effect a miraculous rescue; you must not attempt to originate miracle by your own efforts, especially by any means which savour of magical process. If you do that, at best you will make yourself ridiculous; at the worst, you will put yourself at the disposal of powers that are diabolic, not divine.

And to-day, that attitude is one for which the Church is criticized. It is a commonplace that the

Catholic Church, because she is defending the truth, is constantly having to meet attack from a fresh quarter; her critics, that is to say, are for ever altering their ground. At the Reformation, we Catholics were blamed for attaching too much importance to the action of human free will, for not attaching enough importance to divine grace. To-day, the whole ground of conflict has shifted; we have to defend grace as against free will. At the Reformation, we were accused of neglecting the Bible; to-day, we are reviled for our slavish belief in it. Last century, we were accused of trusting our reason too little; nowadays we are accused of trusting our reason too much. And it is the same in this matter of miracle. Till lately, we had our ecclesiastical miracles criticized on the ground that miracles never happen. To-day, we are having them criticized on the ground that miracles are happening all the time! We, to whom superstition was once imputed, must now defend ourselves against antagonists who take photographs of fairies, and reproduce the voices of the dead on a gramophone record. Is there no pleasing this perpetual insanity of the human mind?

How confidently men assumed, a hundred years ago, that there could be no possible reaction of spirit upon matter! If you came to them with the story that a Saint had been lifted up in the air while in an ecstasy, they would say, "Nonsense, the thing's impossible! The law of gravitation must assert itself. Either there was trickery at work, or your witnesses must have been incompetent witnesses who were the victims of an ocular illusion." To-day, if you tell the same story, you will be met with a quite different answer: "Oh, *that?* Yes, just levitation, of course; a quite recognized phenomenon when the subject is in a state of trance. You will find several cases on record if you consult the Physical Research Society"—and so on. And, not content with capping our own stories of miracle, these Spiritualists and Christian Scientists are very angry with us for not being impressed by theirs. How inconsistent of you (says the Spiritualist) to discredit all our stories of dead men holding communication with the living, when your own Saints have so often appeared in visions! How little you know your own Bible (says the Christian Scientist); don't you realize how absolute a faith in prayer Our Lord demands? Whatsoever thing you shall ask in prayer, it shall be done unto you—don't you see that it is only your lack of faith, your persistent reliance upon human treatment and material medicines, that prevents you from triumphing over disease as we have? All at once we find ourselves in the wrong camp; we, it seems, are the sceptics this time.

Now, the Catholic does not quarrel with these apparently miraculous manifestations outside the Church simply on the ground that they do take place outside the Church. I don't think it is possible to say, off-hand, that a miracle, a real genuine miracle, could not happen among Protestants. We hold, of course, that a genuine miracle could not happen in circumstances which would lead men to suppose that the Protestants were right and the Church was wrong; God cannot but uphold the veracity of His own revelation. But I do not know why a Protestant who is in good faith should not receive a miraculous gift of health even without going to Lourdes. I do not even feel certain that a miracle might not be done to attest the message of some Salvation Army missionary in China, while he was preaching all the faith he knew to men who had no chance of hearing about the faith from Catholic teachers. No, our quarrel both with the Christian Scientists and with the Spiritualists is something different; and it explains not merely why we do not approve of them but why we do not try to imitate them.

We do not approve of them, we do not try to imitate them, because we believe that they are engaged in tempting God. It is one thing to pray for health, even when the doctors have assured you that a restoration of health is impossible. Catholics do that, and believe that such prayers are often wonderfully answered, though whether the answer is strictly miraculous or no they will not pronounce with certainty. It is one thing to trust in Providence, when your duty carries you into danger; to visit the sick, for example, when there is danger of fatal infection. Catholic priests and nuns do that, and Providence is not slow to reward their courage. But it is another thing to deny, defiantly, the whole existence of disease and of pain, to despise all natural remedies and natural precautions. That is what the Christian Scientists invite us to do, at least where they are convinced, at least where they are consistent. For us, to refuse to summon the doctor when a child is lying at death's door is murder, nothing else. You are tempting God by your neglect; and if your neglect seems to be rewarded, it can be no divine miracle which rewards you.

The Spiritualists, too, are tempting God, though after a somewhat different fashion. Man's will is given him by Divine Providence to be the arbiter of his being; in his waking hours, his will must be awake always, he has no right to deaden its action with heavy drinking or with needless taking of drugs. Now, it is one thing to fix this will so firmly upon God that the worshipper seems to pass out of himself altogether, and the body is bereft of its senses, and the mind is open to supernatural revelations; that the Catholic Saints have done. It is quite another thing to abandon your will deliberately to the disposal of some occult powers, you know not what; to leave the fortress of your soul deprived of its captain, and so throw open the gates of it to influences which may, for all you know, be diabolical. Long before Spiritualism was ever thought of, the Church met and settled that difficulty when the Quietists were condemned in the seventeenth century. The Saint in his ecstasy and the medium in his trance may, to all outside observation, look exactly alike; the trance may, for all I know, produce all the strange phenomena of the ecstasy. But they are not the same thing; there is between them the greatest difference in the world, a difference of motive. The mystic abandons his will to God. The medium abandons his will without reservation, and in so abandoning it, he tempts God.

Both the Christian Scientist and the Spiritualist lay claim to what, from the point of view of physical science, seem miracles, just as we do; but there is this difference,—they expect Almighty God to do miracles *to order*. They are presuming upon His grace. And so, because Our Lord refused to cast Himself down from the pinnacle when the devil told Him that Providence would surely save Him from harm; because Our Lord refused to give a sign to the men of his generation precisely when they demanded a sign; because Our Lord would work no miracle precisely when Herod challenged Him to do a miracle, we believe that these modern miracles of Spiritualism and Christian Science are not done in the grace of Christ. And for that reason, we are bound to say that they are not strictly speaking miracles at all. It seems likely enough that, quite apart from that exceptional divine action which we call miracle, nature has mysterious possibilities which Science cannot explain, and probably will never be able to explain. Whether merely human agencies can develop these possibilities at will, or whether it is some diabolic agency that calls them into play, we do not know, and we do not pretend to know. But we do know that we are forbidden to tempt God, and that where God is tempted in the hope of producing a miracle, it is not His power that is set at work, or His voice that makes reply.

Wordsworth, in describing for us the character of the Happy Warrior, tells us that he

"does not stoop, nor lie in wait
For wealth, or honours, or for worldly state;
Whom they must follow, on whose head must fall
Like showers of manna, if they come at all."

And if a hero is one whom worldly honours must
pursue, because he will never lie in wait for them
or make any effort to come by them, shall not we
say the same of the Saint, and of those heavenly
honours with which God sees fit to attest his
sanctity? The Saints have worked miracles, but
they have worked them unreflectively, you might
almost say unwillingly. When St. Philip Neri found
that it was impossible for him to say Mass without
being caught up into an ecstasy which lasted two
or three hours, his first care was to arrange that he
should always say Mass in a private chapel, with
nobody present except one server; there should
be no crowd of sightseers coming to watch Father
Philip's Mass. Can you imagine that a modern
medium, if he found that he involuntarily went
into a trance every day, would observe the same
reticence? No, these modern devotees exploit
miracle, fix their ambition on miracle; and their
results? Let them be what they will, they are not
miracles. God does not dispense with the use of
secondary causes in order to shed lustre upon such
careers as these. It is not that He could not, but

that He would not; that is where our credulity sticks. God grants supernatural favours in His own way, not in ours; they are not to be achieved by so many foot-pounds of prayer; they are not to be secured by creating special conditions under which the phenomena can be regularly produced. They are His surprise presents for His children, and His children know how to take them.

But now, what of our own miracles? We have to admit that phenomena which somewhat resemble the phenomena of sanctity can be produced to-day by men who are not Saints; are produced, therefore, by means which do not altogether transcend the powers of nature, although the secret of them is, and perhaps always will be, undiscoverable. In that case, how can we be sure that our ecclesiastical miracles, or even the miracles recorded in the Gospels, were not similarly produced by occult natural powers? It will not be long, I think, before the Spiritualists re-write in their own jargon the story of Jesus of Nazareth. What answer do we make to such a suggestion as that?

We answer that the charge has already been made, and has already been exploded. It was made in Our Lord's own life-time. "He casteth out devils through Beelzebub, the prince of the devils." Our Lord himself exposed the folly of that suggestion; if it was by Satanic power that He worked, how was it that His power was always used to defeat Satan? The Christian religion has met with magic, in the days of the Apostles and since the days of the Apostles; always it has fought magic and triumphed over it. It has scorned the use of magical appliances; it has refused to put its trust in occult formulas and the apparatus of the curious arts. Where supernatural occurrences have marked its progress, they have come unsolicited, unpremeditated, unlaboriously. If by fifty years' practice you should learn to walk on the sea, you will not have matched the miracle by which St. Peter walked on the sea, in a moment, without preparation, at a word. Whatever miracles you produce, they will be unlike the Christian miracles. They will be unlike the Christian miracles because you have produced them.

BACKGROUND

An objection to miracles was one of the classic arguments against religion made from the eighteenth century onwards. God suspending the natural laws of creation – doing directly what he would generally accomplish by intermediaries – is, or so the argument goes, somehow beneath his dignity, faintly vulgar and show-offish. Knox on the other hand insists that, for him at any rate, the Gospel miracles are necessary for believing that Jesus was indeed God made man. The frequently made argument that someone claiming to be divine must be "mad, bad, or God" is for Knox unpersuasive; only signs of the type promised to accompany the Messiah – miracles of healing, in fact – serve to convince. He also considers miracles happening today, and how they differ from the extraordinary phenomena recorded by spiritualists and parapsychology. Knox's characteristic style combines wit, telling example, and a high degree of logical argument cast into everyday terms.

CTS ONEFIFTIES